E $11.99
Ra   Raffi
             Baby beluga

DATE DUE

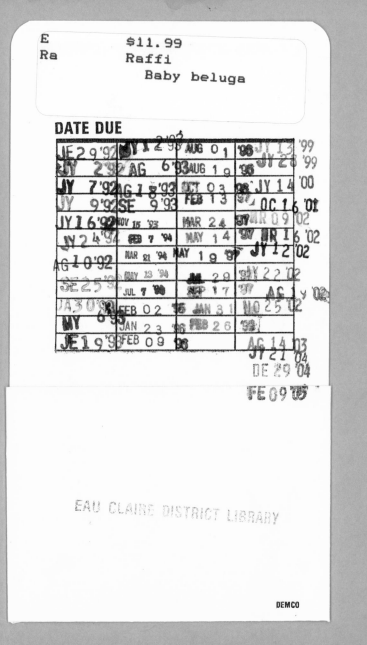

JE 29 '92	JY 12 '93	AUG 0 1 '96	JY 13 '99
JY 2 '92	AG 6 '93	AUG 1 9 '96	JY 28 '99
JY 7 '92	AG 18 '93	OCT 0 3 '96	JY 14 '00
JY 9 '92	SE 9 '93	FEB 13 '97	OC 16 '01
JY 16 '92	NOV 15 '93	MAR 24 '97	MR 09 '02
JY 24 '94	FEB 7 '94	MAY 14 '97	MR 16 '02
AG 10 '92	MAR 21 '94	MAY 19 '97	JY 12 '02
SE 25 '93	MAY 13 '94	JN 29 '97	JY 22 '02
JA 30 '93	JUL 7 '94	SP 17 '97	AG 1 '02
MY 6 '93	FEB 02 '95	JN 31 '98	NO 25 '02
	JAN 23 '96	FEB 26 '98	
JE 19 '93	FEB 09 '96		AG 14 '03
			JY 21 '04
			DE 29 '04
			FE 09 '05

Raffi Songs to Read™

BABY BELUGA

Illustrated by Ashley Wolff

Crown Publishers, Inc., New York

Library of Congress Cataloging-in-Publication Data
Raffi. Baby Beluga / Raffi: Ashley Wolff, illustrator. p.   cm.–(A Raffi
song to read) Summary: Presents the illustrated text to Raffi's song
about the little white whale who swims wild and free. 1. Children's
songs–Texts. [1. Songs. 2. Whales–Fiction.] I. Wolff, Ashley, ill. II. Title.
III. Series: Raffi. Raffi songs to read.
PZ8.3.R124 Bab   1990   89-49367   782.42′0268–dc20   CIP
                                                                  AC
ISBN 0-517-57839-5 (trade)
      0-517-57840-9 (lib. bdg.)

10 9 8 7 6 5 4 3 2 1

First Edition

Front cover photo © David Street
Back cover photo © Patrick Harbron

Baby beluga in the deep blue sea,

Swim so wild and you swim so free.

Heaven above and the sea below,
And a little white whale on the go.

Baby beluga, baby beluga,
Is the water warm? Is your mama home,
With you so happy?

Way down yonder where the dolphins play,

Where you dive and splash all day,
Waves roll in and the waves roll out.

See the water squirtin' out of your spout.

Baby beluga, oh, baby beluga,
Sing your little song, sing for all your friends.

We like to hear you.

When it's dark, you're home and fed.

Curl up snug in your water bed.

Moon is shining and the stars are out.
Good night, little whale, good night.

Baby beluga, oh, baby beluga,
With tomorrow's sun, another day's begun.
You'll soon be waking.

Baby beluga in the deep blue sea,
Swim so wild and you swim so free.

Heaven above and the sea below,
And a little white whale on the go.
You're just a little white whale on the go.

Baby Beluga

Words and music by Raffi and Debi Pike

Ba - by be - lu - ga in the deep blue sea, Swim so wild and you swim so free.

Heav - en a - bove and the sea be - low, And a little white whale on the go.

Ba - by be - lu - ga, ba - by be - lu - ga,

Is the wa - ter warm? Is your ma - ma home, With you so hap - py?

2 Way down yonder where the dolphins play,
   Where you dive and splash all day,
   Waves roll in and the waves roll out.
   See the water squirtin' out of your spout.

   Baby beluga, oh, baby beluga,
   Sing your little song, sing for all your friends.
   We like to hear you.

3 When it's dark, you're home and fed.
   Curl up snug in your water bed.
   Moon is shining and the stars are out.
   Good night, little whale, good night.

   Baby beluga, oh, baby beluga,
   With tomorrow's sun, another day's begun.
   You'll soon be waking.

4 Baby beluga in the deep blue sea,
   Swim so wild and you swim so free.
   Heaven above and the sea below,
   And a little white whale on the go.
   You're just a little white whale on the go.